Sholom's Treasure

How Sholom Aleichem Became a Writer

ERICA SILVERMAN

Pictures by MORDICAI GERSTEIN

Farrar, Straus and Giroux / New York

*To Bel Kaufman, Sholom Aleichem's granddaughter, with thanks for her help
and encouragement*   —E.S.

For my dear uncle, Phillip Chornow   —M.G.

The dialogue in this book is based on Sholom Aleichem's own words as they appear in his
autobiography, *From the Fair.*

Text copyright © 2005 by Erica Silverman
Illustrations copyright © 2005 by Mordicai Gerstein
All rights reserved
Distributed in Canada by Douglas & McIntyre Publishing Group
Color separations by Embassy Graphics
Printed and bound in the United States of America by Phoenix Color Corporation
Typography by Nancy Goldenberg
First edition, 2005
1 3 5 7 9 10 8 6 4 2

www.fsgkidsbooks.com

Library of Congress Cataloging-in-Publication Data
Silverman, Erica.
    Sholom's treasure : how Sholom Aleichem became a writer / Erica Silverman ; pictures by Mordicai
Gerstein.— 1st ed.
       p.   cm.
    Summary: Describes some events in the life of Sholom Aleichem, the Yiddish author who wrote stories
about Jewish life in nineteenth-century Russia.
    ISBN-13: 978-0-374-38055-7
    ISBN-10: 0-374-38055-4
    1. Sholom Aleichem, 1859–1916—Juvenile literature.   2. Authors, Yiddish—19th century—Biography—
Juvenile literature.   3. Jews—Ukraine—Biography—Juvenile literature.   [1. Sholom Aleichem, 1859–1916.
2. Authors, Yiddish.   3. Jews—Biography.]   I. Gerstein, Mordicai, ill.   II. Title.

PJ5129.R2Z845 2005
839'.18309—dc21
[B]
                                                                                                                2002044672

Author's Note

When I was twelve years old, my grandmother took me to a Broadway musical called *Fiddler on the Roof.* Sitting next to her in the darkened theater, I knew I was peering into the world of her childhood. Afterward, I wanted to learn more. "Read Sholom Aleichem," my grandmother told me.

Fiddler on the Roof is based on the stories of Sholom Rabinowitz. This writer, born in Russia in 1859, is best known by his pen name, Sholom Aleichem, a Yiddish greeting that means "Peace be with you."

Sholom Aleichem often set his stories in the shtetl, the small rural village central to nineteenth-century Jewish life in Russia and other parts of eastern Europe. Restricted by law to an isolated, impoverished region known as the Pale of Settlement, Russian Jews were not allowed to own land, enter professions such as law and medicine, or live in cities. Very few Jewish children were permitted to attend Russian schools or universities.

Even though Sholom Aleichem was keenly aware of the hardship and suffering of the people around him, he was able to see the humor in any situation. Believing that laughter was healthy, even necessary, to survival, he made readers laugh at themselves and their problems. At the turn of the century, his stories were read aloud in Jewish homes around the world. To his readers, Sholom Aleichem was a cultural hero.

Sholom knew he should be in bed, but it was Saturday night. Friends and neighbors from all over the small shtetl of Voronko had come to the Rabinowitz home, as always, for the end of the Sabbath. They were eating, drinking, dancing, and singing.

Sholom's eyes were on Father. How lucky they were, he and his brothers, to have such a smart, popular father. Everyone in Voronko looked up to him.

Holding a tattered book in his hands, Father began reading aloud. The guests burst out laughing. Father, his brow usually furrowed with worry, was having a good time. And when Father was happy, Sholom was happy.

Sholom wished he could make people laugh. Maybe someday he would write a book like that one, he thought. Soon he would be starting *kheyder*, Jewish school, where he would learn how to read and write.

When Sholom turned four, Mother walked him to kheyder, told him to study hard, and left him inside the teacher's lopsided one-room hut. Icy air seeped through the cracked walls. Shivering, Sholom noticed that the only warmth came from a wood-burning stove in the far corner of the room. Chickens clucked around the stove. Next to it sat the teacher's wife, mending clothes and rocking a cradle with her foot while keeping an eye on her toddlers, who played nearby.

Sholom sat on a hard bench at a table on the other side of the room. He was squeezed between two bigger boys.

Six days a week, from morning till night, Sholom recited his lessons. Wanting to please his father, he quickly learned the Hebrew alphabet and memorized verses from the Bible.

In time, though, Sholom grew bored. He began to watch the teacher's wife, studying the way she puckered her lips and twitched one eye. Then he turned to his classmates, puckered his lips, and twitched one eye. The boys broke into laughter.

Sholom became known as the class clown. The teacher scolded, smacked, pinched, and whipped him, but once Sholom had found a way to make people laugh, nothing could stop him. His imitations grew more elaborate all the time.

At home, he scrunched up his face, stood on one leg, and rocked back and forth like the rabbi. He whistled through his nose like Yideleh the thief. He licked drops of honey from his fingers like Frumeh the one-eyed maid. He imitated Father's mother, Grandma Minde, talking to God when she prayed.

"He's a monkey," said Mother.

"A scoundrel," said Grandma Minde.

"He'll grow up to be a villain, a bum, a nobody!" predicted Frumeh.

A nobody? Sholom smiled to himself. He had a secret plan. He was going to dig up the treasure buried under the Voronko hill. Everyone had heard of it, but only one person knew how to find it—a poor elderly rabbi who studied magic late into the night.

How did Sholom know this? It happened that his best friend, Shmulik the orphan, lived with this very rabbi and his wife.

Sholom and Shmulik met on the Voronko hillside. "Just how are we going to find the treasure?" Sholom asked Shmulik.

Shmulik's eyes shone. "We must fast for forty days, and each day we must recite forty psalms."

"Which psalms?" Sholom asked.

"If only I knew!" said Shmulik.

Who knew? The rabbi! It was in his secret book, which Shmulik would read as soon as he could spend time alone in the rabbi's study.

Shmulik went on: "When the forty days are up, we sneak out in the dead of night. At the foot of the hill, we each stand on one leg for forty minutes and count forty times forty. If we make no mistakes, the treasure will be ours!"

Sholom planned on giving his share to Father. Whether he was selling wheat or sugar or timber, Father was always worried that business would go bad. With the treasure, Father would smile more. His brow would become smooth. Mother's hands would be soft again, not red and cracked from working all winter in her little shop. And with his own share of the treasure, Shmulik, pale and thin as a reed, wouldn't have to go hungry anymore.

Meanwhile, Sholom divided whatever food he had with his best friend. In return, Shmulik fed Sholom's imagination. He told stories of magic and adventure, filled with wizards, kings, spirits, and wishing stones.

But then the old rabbi died. His widow moved away, taking Shmulik with her. Sholom felt empty and lost.

As time passed, conditions in Russia grew harder. Villagers scrambled to survive. "Make a living? Go squeeze blood from a turnip," Sholom heard someone say. Fewer customers came into Mother's little shop. Friends and neighbors were leaving Voronko to find work elsewhere.

Sholom's parents stopped giving Saturday night parties. Father and Mother whispered behind closed doors. Something was wrong.

Finally, Father gathered the family together. "I have terrible news," he said. "My partner stole my share of the business from under my nose. He left me nothing."

"What will become of us?" Sholom asked.

"We'll start over," said Father. "We'll sell what we can—silverware, goblets, anything of value—and empty Mother's shop. Then we'll move to Pereyaslav."

Pereyaslav! Pereyaslav was almost a city, with wooden sidewalks, cobblestone streets, and buildings that went up three floors!

But Voronko was Sholom's home. His whole world! For eleven years he had trod its dirt roads, swum in its river, breathed its air.

Sholom said goodbye to all of the trees, one by one. Goodbye to the houses and courtyards. Goodbye to the forest and meadow. Goodbye to the bathhouse and the marketplace, the cemetery and the old synagogue.

Sholom came to the foot of the hill and thought about Shmulik. He was sure that someday they would meet again on this very spot. Shmulik would know the forty psalms. Together they would fast for forty days. On a moonless night they would sneak out, unseen, and find the treasure.

Sholom pictured the surprise—and the smile—on Father's face. Shmulik wouldn't have to go away again, and everyone in Voronko would have enough to eat.

Meanwhile, Father and Mother sold all their valuables and bought a run-down inn outside Pereyaslav. Sholom and his sisters and brothers slept on straw mats in a corridor next to the kitchen. The guest rooms held many cots, but hardly any guests.

Mother parceled out stale bread at meals and locked the remainder in a cupboard. Father sighed all the time.

Sholom continued his studies in the crowded, stuffy hut of a new teacher. Chickens clucked around the stove. Goats wandered in and out. Best of all, Sholom found new characters to mimic, and a new audience. He was still a monkey.

On the day of Sholom's bar mitzvah, Father held his head high. Mother looked at Sholom with tears in her eyes. Grandma Minde told him it was time to stop his clowning. He was thirteen years old. According to Jewish law, he was a man.

Two months after Sholom's bar mitzvah, a cholera epidemic spread through town. Mother fell ill.

Sholom watched, frightened, as Grandma Minde did everything the doctor told her to do. He watched as she cried and prayed and pleaded with God.

But early on a Sabbath morning, not long after taking ill, Mother died.

Sholom pressed his face into his pillow and wept. Hearing Father's sobs, he cried harder.

For the seven days of mourning, Sholom, his brothers and sisters, Father, and Grandma Minde sat on the floor. Friends and family came and went, bringing food and kind words. One visitor was Father's brother, Uncle Pinney.

"What will I do? What will I do?" Father kept saying.

"You'll do what every Jew does," Uncle Pinney told him. "You'll marry again."

Father could not imagine marrying anyone else. Besides, who would want a man with twelve children?

"A man needs a wife," Uncle Pinney argued.

In time, Father and Uncle Pinney hatched a plan. They sent six of the children to relatives far away. Kept hidden until Father found a new wife, the six children called themselves "the secret merchandise."

The new wife arrived to find herself with twelve stepchildren. She was furious. Although she spoke respectfully to Father and Grandma Minde, she lashed out at the children with whippings and sharp words. When they cried, she teased them. She had her own mocking name for each one. Sholom she called Pupik, bellybutton.

Now there were endless chores. In all kinds of weather, Sholom had to stand outside for hours at a time, calling to travelers to stop at the inn.

One freezing day, Sholom peered down the desolate road, stamping his feet to keep warm. How he longed to bring home a large group of well-to-do merchants. What a present that would be for Father! The well-dressed guests would emerge from a fancy carriage and follow him inside. Father would greet them, smiling. "Each one wants his own room," Sholom would tell Father. "Will they stay for the Sabbath?" "Of course! Maybe even until the next Sabbath, and the next."

The clip-clop of hooves interrupted Sholom's daydream. A carriage was heading his way. Sholom waved. He jumped up and down. "Here! Stop here!" he called out.

But the wagon flew by, spraying snow in his face. It stopped down the road at Yasnogradsky's Inn, which had large rooms, fine furniture, and always the best customers.

Sholom trudged home. His brothers and sisters were scrubbing walls, sweeping floors, peeling potatoes, chopping onions. "The stepmother," as he referred to her, was snarling at one and smacking another.

Seeing Sholom, she turned abruptly and scowled. "You couldn't get even one guest? Pupik! Good-for-nothing! What do you do all day, sleep?"

Sholom was silent.

"Because of you, the fish I cooked will go to waste." She eyed him suspiciously. "Or maybe you thought you could have some? Ha! I'll throw it away before I give you one bite."

Sholom ran back outside.

"Run! Run yourself ragged!" she screamed after him.

Sholom hated the stepmother's constant scolding, but he was fascinated by her curses and her clever way with words. *Eat? May worms eat you! Yell? Yell your teeth out! Sleep? Sleep on live coals!* Sometimes she cursed in rhyme: *May you ache and break! Peak and pine and split your spine!* Even her names for others amused him: *Oaf, Dunderhead, Pimple, Pipsqueak.*

Sholom began to write these down. He organized them into a "dictionary." He titled this work "The Sharp Tongue of the Stepmother." Every night, he added to it and rewrote the entire book to keep it in alphabetical order.

One night, Father came in. He picked up Sholom's dictionary and started to read.

Sholom sat frozen. Without a word, Father left.

After a while, Sholom heard murmuring. Father was reading the dictionary aloud. To the stepmother! Sholom waited, terrified.

Suddenly the stepmother laughed! She laughed so hard she woke the whole house. Everyone thought she would laugh herself to death. And the cause? It was something he—Sholom the pupik—had written! With humor, what could he not accomplish?

At kheyder, Sholom used humor to battle a bully, a boy who was rich, mean, and arrogant.

To show off, the boy wore his expensive winter boots year-round. On rainy days, he held out his feet expectantly as Yankel the beggar and Laybel the widow's son removed the boots and wiped off the sticky mud with their bare hands. Sometimes he tossed them a penny.

Sholom hated seeing this. He mimicked the bully and teased the boys.

Finally, with the few pennies he'd earned doing errands, he bought bagels to bribe the boys, saying, "You must never bow down to Mr. Boots again."

To teach the bully a lesson, Sholom hid his boots. The rich boy cried to his father. His father ordered the teacher to kick Sholom out of kheyder.

"Sholom is a troublemaker," the teacher admitted. "But kick him out? Not a chance! He's my smartest student!"

Father's friends also thought Sholom was very smart. One, known as the Collector because he collected money for lottery tickets, lent Sholom some difficult books.

"Maybe he can read the words," said Sholom's father, "but does he really understand the meaning?"

"Why shouldn't he?" the Collector replied, adding, "Well, maybe some books are above his head—the novels of Abraham Mapu, for instance."

His curiosity roused, Sholom secretly borrowed a thick Mapu novel from Father's shelves. He finished it overnight and was gripped by a desire to write.

Stitching papers together to make a book, he stayed awake night after night, writing by the light of a kerosene lamp.

One night, the stepmother burst in on him. "Leech! Cockroach!" she said. "Burn up our kerosene, will you? You should burn with fever!" She tore some pages from his book and turned to toss them into the fireplace.

Just in time, Father hurried in and snatched the pages from her hands. He read Sholom's book, and the next day he gave it to the Collector.

Days passed. Sholom waited nervously. What would Father's friend say?

"Come here, you rascal," the Collector said finally. He pinched Sholom's cheeks. To Father, he announced, "This boy is going to be a somebody. Mark my words!"

Some days later, as Father was chanting his morning prayers in the kitchen, Sholom paced back and forth, memorizing a poem for school.

"I suppose the young scholar thinks he's too good to lift a finger," the stepmother complained. "Would it break his back to pick up a samovar and fill it with water for tea?"

Father stopped chanting. "No more! I will not allow it!" he shouted.

The stepmother looked stunned.

Father continued: "From now on, you may not order this boy about. You must leave him alone. Sholom is special!"

For a long time, nobody spoke, not even the stepmother. Then Father went back to his prayers.

Sholom smiled to himself. So! He was going to be a somebody. He knew exactly what that meant. He was going to be a writer.

That was the treasure Sholom would give Father.

Afterword

Sholom Aleichem gave his father and the world more than six thousand stories, essays, plays, and novels. Drawing on his own life for much of his work, he wrote stories set in Kasrilevke, a shtetl like Voronko.

Although he spoke Russian and Hebrew, Sholom Aleichem chose Yiddish for most of his writing. He believed passionately that Yiddish best captured the essence of eastern European Jewish culture, and he worked hard to keep it alive.

Sholom Aleichem died in New York City on May 13, 1916. More than a hundred thousand people lined the streets as his funeral procession passed by, many crying as if they'd lost a close friend.

In his will, Sholom Aleichem asked that his name "be recalled with laughter."

Sources

BOOKS

Aleichem, Sholem. *From the Fair: The Autobiography of Sholem Aleichem.* Ed. and trans. Curt Leviant. New York: Viking Penguin, 1985.

Aleichem, Sholom. *The Great Fair: Scenes from My Childhood.* Trans. Tamara Kahana. Illus. Marc Chagall. New York: Noonday Press, 1955.

Grafstein, M. W. (Melech). *Sholom Aleichem Panorama.* Ontario, Canada: Jewish Observer, 1948.

Rabinowitz, Wolf (Vevik). *Mayn Bruder Sholem-Aleykhem: Zikhroynes.* Kiev, Ukraine: Melukhe-Farlag Far di Natsyonale Minderhaytn in USSR, 1939.

Waife-Goldberg, Marie. *My Father, Sholom Aleichem.* New York: Simon & Schuster, 1968.

ARCHIVAL MATERIAL

Letter to Ravnitzki from Sholom Aleichem. October 1904. YIVO Archives.